First published in Great Britain in 2009 by Buster Books,
an imprint of Michael O'Mara Books Limited,
9 Lion Yard, Tremadoc Road, London SW4 7NQ

Written by Sarah Stewart and Abigail Keen
Illustrated by Katy Jackson
Created and produced by Toucan Books
3rd Floor, 89 Charterhouse Street, London EC1M 6HR
Production by Joanne Rooke
Cover by Zoe Quayle (from a design by www.blacksheep-uk.com)
Cover illustration by Paul Moran

A CIP catalogue record for this book is available from the British Library

ISBN: 978-1-906082-55-0

2 4 6 8 10 9 7 5 3 1

www.mombooks.com/busterbooks

Printed and bound in Italy by Rotolito Lombarda

Papers used by Buster Books are natural, recyclable products made from wood grown in sustainable forests. The manufacturing processes conform to the environmental regulations of the country of origin.

The GIRLS' Annual 2010

Buster Books

Contents

It's A Girls' World

It is really fantastic being a girl.

Boys miss out on so much! We get to chat to our friends about everything, organize sleepovers, paint our nails, style our hair, wear cool clothes. The list of the fun that girls can have is endless.

And that's what this book is all about.

Turn the pages to discover quizzes, stories, things to make, recipes to try, and games to play with your friends. You can even learn how to introduce yourself in different languages. Just take a look at the page opposite.

Talk To Girls Around The World

Have you ever wanted to speak in a different language? Learn the simple phrases below and you'll be able to make friends with girls like you in other countries.

GERMANY
Hello **Guten Tag** (goot-en tahk)
Goodbye **Auf Wiedersehen** (owf-vee-dair-zayn)
Please **Bitte** (bih-tuh)
Thank you **Danke** (dahn-kuh)

ITALY
Hello **Buongiorno** (bwon-jor-no)
Goodbye **Arrivederci** (ah-ree-vuh-dehr-chee)
Please **Per favore** (pehr fah-voh-reh)
Thank you **Grazie** (graht-zee-eh)

SPAIN
Hello **¡Hola!** (oh-lah)
Goodbye **¡Adiós!** (ah-dee-ohs)
Please **Por favor** (por fah-bor)
Thank you **Gracias** (grah-see-ahs)

FRANCE
Hello **Bonjour** (bon-joor)
Goodbye **Au revoir** (oh ruh-vwar)
Please **S'il vous plaît** (seel voo play)
Thank you **Merci** (mer-see)

GREECE
Hello **Γειά σου** (yia-so)
Goodbye **Αντίο** (and-ee-oh)
Please **Παρακαλῶ** (parakalo)
Thank you **Ευχαριστώ** (ef-ha-ree-sto)

NETHERLANDS
Hello **Hallo** (hah-loh)
Goodbye **Tot ziens** (toht zeens)
Please **Alstublieft** (ahlst-ew-bleeft)
Thank you **Dank u wel** (dahnk ew vehl)

JAPAN
Hello **Konnichi wa** (kon-nee-chee wah)
Goodbye **Sayonara** (sa-yoh-nah-rah)
Please **Kudasai** (ku-dah-sa-i)
Thank you **Domo arigato** (doh-moh ah-ree-gah-toh)

Go-Girl Quiz

Did you know that your interests can reveal lots about your personality?
Take the quiz below to find out if you are a busy bee or a chilled-out chick.

1. What's your idea of a brilliant Saturday?

A. Sleeping late, then catching up on all your favourite TV shows.
B. A whole day shopping with your best mates, only stopping for milk shakes.
C. A sunny day – you can be outside all day long. You hate to be stuck indoors.

2. When you leave school, you'd love to be …

A. A bass player, so you get to be in a famous band, but not centre stage.
B. A famous actress with a personal hairstylist, who goes everywhere with you.
C. An Olympic sprinter or top footballer – and beat all the boys!

3. What are your favourite colours?

A. Dark colours such as purple, navy and black.
B. Pastel colours such as pink, yellow and baby blue.
C. Vibrant colours such as red, orange and gold.

4. Your school holds a fair to raise money for charity. How do you show your support?

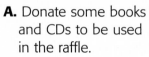
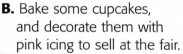

A. Donate some books and CDs to be used in the raffle.
B. Bake some cupcakes, and decorate them with pink icing to sell at the fair.
C. Organize a sponsored run around the school field.

5. Which shopping list suits your style best?

A. A rock-chick T-shirt, cool bracelets and a selection of hair accessories.
B. A sparkly pink top, a pair of jeans and some pretty ballet pumps.
C. A cosy hoodie and some new trainers that everyone will love.

6. If you could pick any of these cute pets, which one would you like?

A. A puppy, so you could take him on quiet walks.
B. A cuddly kitten, because they are so sweet and strokeable.
C. A gorgeous pony, so you could go out riding every single day.

7. You see an audition poster for the school play. What do you do?

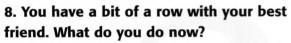

A. Don't go to the audition, but sign up to help behind the scenes.

B. Go along with your best friends and hope to get a part.

C. Feel really excited and start to learn the lines for the star role.

8. You have a bit of a row with your best friend. What do you do now?

A. Feel sad, then decide to make her a cool CD, so you'll be mates again in no time.

B. Sulk for a bit, then go and make up with a hug. You can't be cross for long.

C. Phone her up immediately to clear the air.

9. Your birthday is coming up. How would you most like to spend it?

A. Going to see a cool movie with one or two close friends. Big parties just aren't your thing.

B. Inviting a group of your best friends round for a fun and girly sleepover.

C. Hiring out your local leisure centre and throwing a swimming party for everyone in your class.

10. A girl you don't know falls over in the playground. What do you do?

A. Ask her if she's OK and then stand back so she doesn't feel embarrassed.

B. Go up to her and give her a hug.

C. Run to get help from a teacher.

Now it's time to work out what your answers say about you. Grab a pencil and some paper. Note down how many As, Bs and Cs you got, then turn to page 60.

Are you too much of an on-the-go girl to tidy your room? Turn to page 41 for tips.

❁Ribbon Hair Band❁

Looking stylish has never been so much fun. For a cute and original hairstyle, simply follow the instructions below. This pretty ribbon hair band will guarantee you never have another bad hair day. Decorate it any way you like, with beads, buttons, glitter or feathers. It's up to you.

You Will Need:

* A flexible tape measure
* A plain hair-elastic
* Ribbon
* Scissors
* Needle and thread
* Felt in different colours
* A button

1 Measure around your head with a flexible tape measure.

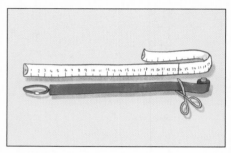

2 Now cut a piece of ribbon that length, minus the length of your hair elastic, as shown above.

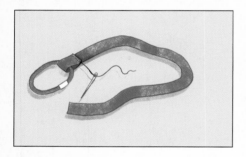

3 Fold one end of the ribbon around one side of your hair elastic. Stitch to hold it in place.

4 Repeat with the other end of the ribbon, sewing it to the opposite side of the elastic.

5 To decorate your hair band, cut out two flower shapes from felt, one slightly smaller than the other.

6 Put the small flower on top of the large one, then position a pretty button in the middle.

7 Place your flower on the band opposite the elastic. Sew through the button and all the layers, to attach.

TOP TIP: To stop your hair band slipping off, wrap two small pieces of felt around the ribbon, either side of the hair elastic. Then sew these into place.

8 Now your hair band is ready to wear. You can tie your hair up at the back for added style or leave it down for a natural look.

Making things yourself is fun!

Top Tips

✴ To make a hair band more quickly, but less neatly, cut the ribbon a little longer and tie the ends around your hair elastic in knots, instead of sewing them into place.

✴ Look out for sparkly, patterned or fancy ribbon to make extra-special hair bands.

✴ Try using differently coloured felt or patterned fabrics for the flower. Why not combine spots and stripes?

Alternatives

If flowers aren't for you, or if you want to make a few different bands, try some of these alternatives.

Sew buttons or sequins all along the length of the hair band.

Make a cute bow from felt or fabric, and sew or glue it on to the hair band at one side.

Add sparkle to a wide ribbon hair band with spots of glitter glue.

Push the ribbon through two or three beads, before you stitch the ribbon to the elastic.

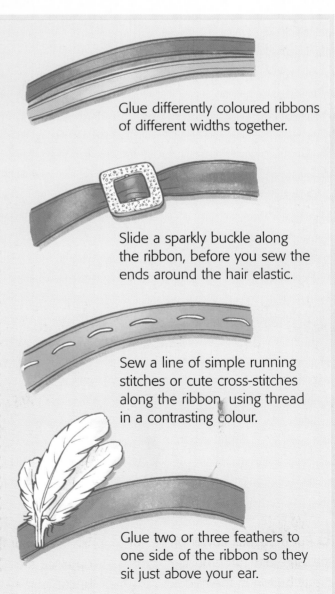

Glue differently coloured ribbons of different widths together.

Slide a sparkly buckle along the ribbon, before you sew the ends around the hair elastic.

Sew a line of simple running stitches or cute cross-stitches along the ribbon, using thread in a contrasting colour.

Glue two or three feathers to one side of the ribbon so they sit just above your ear.

⭐ Backstage Drama ⭐

Summer couldn't believe her luck. It was the first day of the school holidays, and she was about to go backstage at the Royal National Theatre. She took a deep breath and opened the double doors. As she stepped inside, a glamorous woman with long brown hair and high heels charged towards her.

'I told them I want lilies in my dressing room, NOT roses!' the woman shouted into her mobile, pushing Summer out the way.

Summer gasped, but the woman carried on walking through the doors. It was Jenny Curzon, one of the most famous actresses in the world. Summer was shocked by how rude she was.

'Summer Andrews?' a boy with messy hair interrupted her thoughts. He was carrying a clipboard and had a nice smile.

'Yes, that's me,' Summer answered. 'Sorry, I got distracted.'

'Met Jenny Curzon, did you?' the boy winked. 'She's trouble. But she gets away with it, of course. The play needs her.'

Summer nodded and straightened her T-shirt.

'Right. Well my name is John, and I've been told to show you to the wardrobe department to help. How does that sound?'

'Great!' Summer grinned, feeling instantly better.

'I was hoping I would get to help with the costumes.'

That afternoon, Summer spent a fantastic couple of hours helping Amanda, the wardrobe mistress.

'You're doing brilliantly,' smiled Amanda, as Summer finished the final dress. 'I just need to pop out – can I leave you to arrange those hats over there?'

'Sure!' Summer said. This was even more fun than she'd expected.

Amanda left the room, and Summer started to attach ribbon to the hats. Suddenly the door flew open and John sprinted in, looking worried.

'Where's Amanda?' he asked, out of breath. 'We've got a problem. Jenny Curzon hates her outfit for the play. She's refusing to go on stage if we don't fix it.'

'What?' gasped Summer. 'That's crazy! Amanda's gone out – she said she'd be back in an hour.'

'That's no good. We need someone to fix this now!' John cried. He ran his hands through his messy hair, making it stick up even more than it had before.

Summer bit her lip. If there was no show, all those people who'd bought tickets would be so disappointed. Her heart was hammering. 'What if I try to fix the dress?' she said.

John's eyes lit up, 'It's worth a try. Come on!' He grabbed Summer's hand and they ran out into the corridor.

Summer could hear Jenny Curzon shouting from behind the closed dressing-room door.

'OK,' said John. 'You can do this.' He squeezed Summer's hand tightly, but she could tell he was nervous. They knocked on the door.

'What do you want?' snapped Jenny, as she opened the door. Her dark eyes flashed, and she scowled at the two young people in front of her.

'I … I think I can help you,' Summer said nervously. She swallowed. 'We have a dark-blue dress in the wardrobe department. I can make some changes to it, so that it looks really nice.'

Jenny Curzon sniffed. 'Well, you can try,' she said. 'But if I don't like it, I won't be going on stage.' Then she slammed the door in Summer's face.

'I'd better get started,' yelled Summer as she sprinted off down the corridor.

'I hope you know what you're doing,' called John.

Summer hoped so too.

Summer had never worked so fast in her life. She sewed on black-lace sleeves and tied a beautiful silk sash around the waist. In just 50 minutes, she had transformed the dress – but what would Jenny think? She ran back towards her dressing room and knocked on the door. When Jenny answered, she took the dress and said nothing.

'Oh no!' thought Summer.

Then Jenny smiled. 'You've done a beautiful job,' she said, and then, to Summer's surprise. 'Thank you.'

Summer smiled back and let out a huge sigh of relief. Just as she turned to go, Jenny stopped her.

'Wait,' she said. 'I think you deserve a gift – especially as I was so rude before. Let's see … which would you prefer – the use of my limousine for the rest of the evening, a shopping spree in your favourite store, or three pairs of tickets for the show next week? It's sold out, you know.'

Summer was amazed. Which one should she go for? It's up to you! Turn the page and choose …

You Choose The Ending …

LIMOUSINE

Summer's best friends, Katie and Lucy, arrived at the theatre, and the three girls each chose a dress from the wardrobe department. When they were ready, John walked them to Jenny's limo and politely opened the door.

'You did a fantastic job today Summer,' he said shyly. He blushed. 'And you look really pretty in your dress.'

When the limo drove off, Katie grabbed Summer's hand. 'Was this the craziest day of your life or what?'

Summer grinned. Working backstage was so much fun!

SHOPPING

Summer, Katie and Lucy ran around their favourite shop collecting piles of gorgeous clothes.

'That is perfect on you,' breathed Lucy, as Summer tried on a bright-red dress with leggings and ballet pumps. 'You have to get it!'

Summer grinned at her reflection. 'I think I will,' she announced and flicked her hair behind her ears like Jenny Curzon. Her friends giggled so much they couldn't stop.

Later, they agreed it had been the best day ever.

TICKETS

The next week, Summer sat in the best seat in the house. Katie and Lucy were waving at her from the theatre box opposite, with big smiles on their faces. Her mum and dad were there too, giving her a thumbs up. Then Summer looked to her left and grinned. Sitting next to her was John – and he'd even combed his hair for the occasion!

'Thanks Summer,' he whispered. 'I've always wanted to see the show from up here. You're a friend for life.'

Summer just smiled. She couldn't believe working backstage at the theatre could be so dramatic.

Maze In A Mall

This lost girl is trying to find the record store, shoe shop, and fashion shop. Can you help her? She needs to start from the mall entrance each time. Answers on page 60.

Rocky-Road Bars

Cooking is a lot of fun, and a great skill to learn. Try it for yourself by making this tasty snack. Gather the ingredients below and follow the steps to make 12 delicious chocolate bars filled with marshmallows and cherries. Be sure to treat your friends!

INGREDIENTS

300 g milk or plain chocolate
100 g butter
1 tbsp golden syrup
150 g digestive biscuits
100 g mini marshmallows
40 g glacé cherries, halved
40 g roughly chopped nuts (optional)

Warning

Always ask an adult for help if you are using a stove and boiling water. You want to melt the ingredients, not your fingers!

1 Line a 20-cm-square cake tin with non-stick baking paper.

2 Half fill a saucepan with water and bring to the boil.

3 Break up the chocolate and put it into a large heat-proof bowl.

4 Rest the bowl on top of the saucepan, above the boiling water.

5 Add the butter and golden syrup, then stir until melted into the chocolate. Remove the pan from the heat and allow the mixture to cool.

6 Break the biscuits into small pieces and stir into the chocolate mixture.

7 Add the marshmallows, cherries and nuts (if using) and stir until everything is completely covered.

8 Pour into the prepared tin and press down with the back of a spoon until flat. Then chill in the fridge.

9 Chill for at least two hours, then turn out of the tin and cut into 12 tasty bars.

Nuts

Don't add nuts to your Rocky-Road Bars if you or your friends are allergic. Always ask first if you are unsure. For an alternative option you can always try raisins, sultanas or even coconut shavings. These will taste just as delicious as nuts.

Cupcake Queen

These cupcakes have been cooling on a tray and are ready for decorating. Grab some colourful pens and make them look extra delicious – add hearts or stars, write your name or initials – it's up to you.

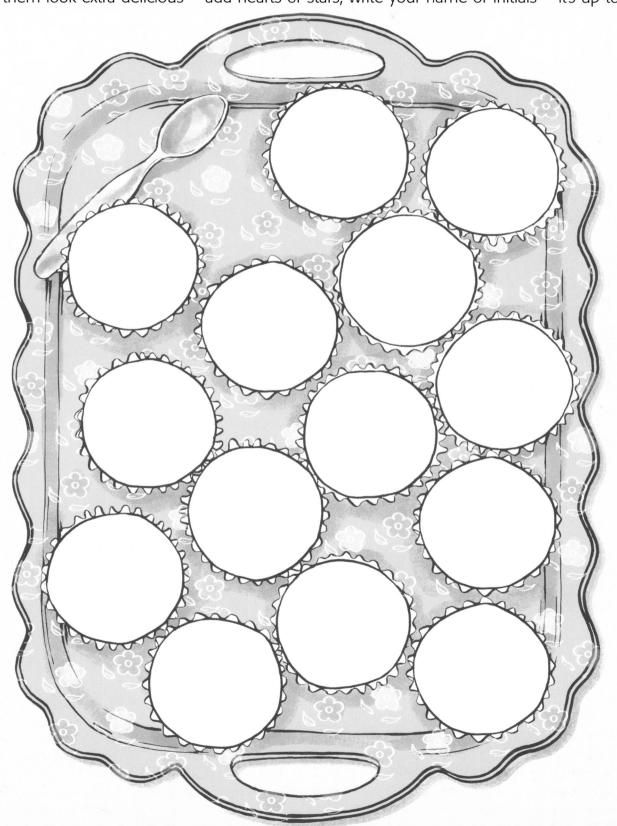

Wonder Women

Read all about three incredibly brave women who changed the world.

> I never ran my train off the track, and I never lost a passenger.
>
> HARRIET TUBMAN

Harriet Tubman

Harriet Tubman was born into slavery in the USA in 1820. As a slave she had to work long hours with no pay and was often beaten or whipped. When she was 30 years old she couldn't stand the horrible conditions anymore, so she planned her escape. It was dangerous but, with the help of friends, she survived.

After she was free from slavery, Harriet Tubman rescued other members of her family, and she wanted to help others. Over the next ten years, she led hundreds of slaves to freedom using an 'Underground Railroad'. This was a secret route across America, with a network of safe houses or 'stations' for slaves to rest in. Harriet was known as a 'conductor', who guided slaves along the route towards Canada, where they could live as free people. Reward posters were put up for every slave Harriet helped escape, but none was ever caught.

WANTED
$300 REWARD
FOR RUNAWAY SLAVES

She became known as the 'Moses of her people', because her work was compared to the biblical figure who safely led slaves out of Egypt. Later in life, she became a leader in the campaign to abolish slavery. She was an amazing woman who never gave up.

MORE AMAZING WOMEN

- **Jane Austen** is one of the world's greatest novelists. Born in England in 1775, her books, including *Emma* and *Pride and Prejudice,* are still enjoyed by millions of people today.
- **Emmeline Pankhurst** formed the suffragettes in 1898, to campaign for a woman's right to vote. She was sent to prison, but she never gave up, and the vote was won in England in 1918.
- **Marie Curie** was a brilliant scientist, and her work on radioactivity in 1903 paved the way for the treatment of cancer. She was the first person to receive two Nobel Prizes.
- **Rosalind Franklin** helped uncover the structure of DNA in the 1950s. She used a special X-ray technique to take photographs of molecules, and this led others to the amazing discovery.

Gladys Aylward

Gladys Aylward was born in London in 1902, and grew up working as a parlour maid. She was a very religious woman and wanted to dedicate her life to serving God. When she was 30, she left for China because she believed God was calling her to preach Christianity's message to the Chinese people.

Two years after Gladys arrived in China, the people in the city of Yangchen had begun to know and respect her. One day, the Mandarin of Yangchen asked Gladys to stop a riot in the prison. Gladys listened to the prisoners and they stopped fighting. From then on she became known as 'Ai-weh-deh,' which means 'Virtuous one'.

Gladys opened orphanages in China, where she cared for children until her death in 1970. During World War Two, she helped guide 100 orphans to a safe place. She led them across mountains and rivers for 12 days, until they reached an orphanage in the city of Sian. She is remembered as a brave and peaceful woman, who always wanted to do good.

❝ The thought of China tormented me. God wanted me there. ❞

GLADYS AYLWARD

Violette Szabo

Violette Szabo's husband, an officer in the French army, was killed in 1942 during World War Two. His death upset Violette so much, that she volunteered to become a spy to help fight the Nazis.

Violette joined the Special Operations Executive (SOE), and after lots of difficult training, she was parachuted into France on 5 April, 1944. The Allies' spy network had been broken up in the area by the Germans, but when Violette landed, she reorganized it. Her first mission was a success and she uncovered lots of very important information.

However, when she was sent to France in June 1944 on another mission, she was captured by the enemy. Tragically, Violette died a few months later, aged just 23. After her death, she was awarded the George Cross. She is remembered as a courageous woman and a true heroine.

☯ Stretch It Out ☯

Yoga is an ancient and spiritual exercise. It energizes the entire body and, because it is so relaxing, it is very healthy for the mind, too. If you have had a stressful day, or if you just feel like trying something new, why not have a go at these basic stretches?

CHILD'S POSE

1. Kneel on the floor and put your feet together so that your big toes are touching.
2. Sit back on your heels, then slowly breathe out and lean forward until your head gently touches the floor.
3. Bring your arms back alongside your thighs. Make sure your hands are resting with the palms face up.
4. Relax like this for 30 seconds.

DID YOU KNOW?

Yoga is thought to have originated in India about 5,000 years ago. It has roots in Buddhism and Hinduism, but it is described as a spiritual science, and not as a religion. When you practise yoga, you learn how to feel relaxed.

This is a peaceful pose. Can you do it?

CROSS-LEGGED MEDITATION POSE

1. Sit on the floor with crossed legs.
2. Straighten your back and take a slow, deep breath.
3. Pull your shoulders up to your ears and ease them back down again. You should now be feeling nice and relaxed.
4. Sit like this for 30 seconds, taking slow breaths.

TREE POSE

1. Stand on your right foot and balance. Now bend your left knee.
2. Slowly, reach down with your left hand and take hold of your left ankle.
3. Pull your foot up very gently, and place the sole against the inside of your thigh.
4. Straighten your back and keep balancing.
5. Place both hands together as shown in the picture. Hold this position for 30 seconds, breathing slowly.

Your legs should be stretched and your chest should feel open.

TRIANGLE POSE

1. Stand with your feet wide apart and facing forwards.
2. Turn your left foot out to a 90 degree angle.
3. Now breathe out and lean over your left leg, bending at the hip. Take your time.
4. Keep your left leg straight and slowly stretch your left hand down towards the floor as far as you can. Rest your hand on your leg.
5. Stretch your right arm up in the air.
6. If it feels comfortable, turn your head to the right, so you look up at your right hand.
7. Keep balancing. See if you can manage this pose for 30 seconds. It's a bit trickier than the others.

LOTUS FLOWER

The lotus grows in muddy water. You can find it in ponds and lagoons in exotic countries, such as China and India. In Yoga, it is seen as a symbol of purity, because the beautiful petals open just above the dirty surface of the water. The buds close at night, so the flower stays safe, dry and pretty.

DOWNWARD-FACING DOG

1. Get on the floor on your hands and knees.
2. Slowly rise up so you make a triangle shape with your feet flat on the floor and your palms flat too, head facing downwards.
3. Now breathe out and straighten your legs and arms. Keep your head between your upper arms, don't let it hang down.
4. Stay in this position for 30 seconds.

This pose is very good for your back.

Breathe slowly and focus on your posture.

MOUNTAIN POSE

1. Stand up straight with your big toes just touching, and arms by your sides.
2. Rock gently back and forth and side to side, then find a comfortable balance.
3. Let your arms hang loose and relaxed beside your body.
4. Stay in this position for 30 seconds to one minute, breathing easily.

The Spooky Bus

It was lunchtime at school and Kate, Lydia and Amanda were sitting on their favourite picnic bench in the playground.

'Do you want to know a secret?' Kate asked her two best friends. She leaned in and whispered, 'The school bus is haunted.'

Lydia's brown eyes widened, but Amanda frowned. 'I don't believe in ghosts,' she said.

'It's true,' Kate flicked her dark hair over her shoulder. 'Billy Holden told me. Sometimes, when it's quiet, you can hear laughter. It's really creepy.'

'That's terrifying,' Lydia said and gasped. 'Oh no! I have to get the bus tomorrow because Dad can't take me.'

'Don't worry Lydia,' Amanda interrupted. 'Kate's making it up.'

'I am not!' Kate crossed her arms in a huff. 'You should get the bus tomorrow. Then you would believe me.'

'Fine,' said Amanda. 'I will.'

> There was a low rumbling sound. Lydia gasped and looked up at the black clouds in the sky.

The next morning, the three friends waited at the bus stop. Kate and Lydia were nervous, but Amanda was rolling her eyes. Five minutes went by, and then there was a low rumbling sound. Lydia gasped and looked up at the black clouds in the sky. Was there going to be a thunderstorm? At that moment, the old bus appeared at the top of the hill, its engine growling.

'Shall we turn back?' Lydia asked. 'I think we should turn back.'

'Don't be silly,' said Amanda. 'It's perfectly fine. The bus is not haunted.'

'That's what you think,' Kate muttered.

The bus screeched to a halt and the doors opened. It was so dark inside, that Lydia could only just see the driver. Kate and Amanda stepped on. Lydia gulped and followed them to the middle row of seats.

'See, this isn't so bad, is it Lydia?' Amanda said as they sat down.

'Just you wait,' Kate's eyes gleamed. 'It always starts off fine, but after a while, you start to hear the ghostly laughter.'

'Stop it!' Amanda shouted. 'Can't you see Lydia's really scared?'

'So am I,' Kate shouted back. 'You should be too.'

The bus pulled off with a creak and Lydia's heart thumped loudly in her chest.

'Well, there's nothing to be scared of,' Amanda started saying. 'It's just an old bus, that's all. So it will make a bit of a noise, and …'

'HAHAHAHAHAHA!'

All three girls froze.

'Did you hear that?' Kate whispered.

Lydia felt like she was going to cry. She clutched at Amanda's arm, and Amanda clutched back.

When the bus stopped outside the school gates, all three girls jumped up and ran. The doors screeched open and they all raced onto the pavement.

'OK, I believe you,' Amanda said to Kate once they were outside. 'There was definitely someone laughing. It was really creepy.'

'Told you,' Kate said.

'We should do something about it,' Amanda continued. She thought for a moment, 'I think I've got a plan, but we're going to have to be brave and get back on the bus. You too, Lydia.'

> Lydia felt like she was going to cry. She clutched at Amanda's arm, and Amanda clutched back.

Lydia nodded, but she didn't feel very brave.

That evening, the girls were ready to put Amanda's plan into action. Even Lydia was feeling better as the bus stopped to let them on outside school. They climbed on and headed for the middle row, their classmates following in a noisy line.

'Remember,' Amanda said. 'Wait for the laughter.'

The bus drove off, and sure enough, the girls heard the laughter again.

'HAHAHAHAHA!'

But this time was different. Instead of being scared, the girls were ready.

'NOW!' Amanda shouted and they jumped up.

'NO GHOSTS! GO AWAY!' All three yelled as loud as they could.

To their surprise, the laughter continued, but this time it wasn't creepy. It sounded normal, and was coming from the back of the bus.

'HAHA! So funny! HAHAHA!' It was Billy Holden. He was clutching his sides and pointing at them.

Amanda folded her arms, Lydia's mouth dropped open, and Kate frowned. All three girls suddenly realized there was no ghost. Just Billy and his games. The spooky school bus wasn't so spooky after all.

Princess Slippers

On a cold winter evening, a pair of slippers will keep your feet nice and cosy, and they look super cute, too. Follow the steps below to make some of your own. All you need is a pair of warm socks, some ribbon and a handful of pretty beads for decoration.

You Will Need:

* Thick, fluffy socks
* Scissors
* Narrow ribbon
* A needle with a large eye
* A selection of chunky beads

1 Snip a row of tiny holes or slits, roughly 2 cm below the top edge of each sock.

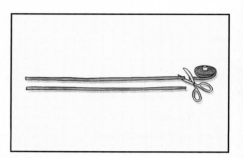

2 Cut two pieces of narrow ribbon, each 75 cm long, one for each sock.

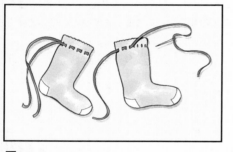

3 Thread the ribbon through a large needle, and take it in-and-out through the sock holes. Then remove the needle.

4 Tie the ribbon in a bow at the back of each sock, and trim off the long ends.

5 Thread beads onto the ends of the ribbons, again using a needle to make it easier.

6 Tie small knots at the ends of the ribbons to stop the beads from falling off.

7 Now you have a beautiful pair of princess slippers.

ALTERNATIVES

* Cut some ribbon into short lengths and tie into lots of tiny bows. Glue or stitch these in a row down the fronts or sides of the socks.
* Snip two rows of holes down one side of each sock, instead of along the top. Thread ribbon between the holes to create a laced, criss-cross effect, and tie in a bow at the top edge.

Midnight Snack

Home-made biscuits are so much yummier than those you buy in the supermarket, and baking them is lots of fun, too. This recipe will make 20 oatmeal and raisin cookies – perfect for a midnight snack. Why not have a sleepover and share them with your friends?

INGREDIENTS

50 g raisins
3 tbsp orange juice
100 g self-raising flour
150 g rolled oats
75 g light muscovado
  sugar
75 g butter
1 tbsp golden syrup

SAFETY TIP:
Ask an adult to help you when using the hob and the oven. These get very hot.

1 Preheat the oven to 350°F/180°C/Gas Mark 4.

2 Lightly grease two baking sheets with a thin layer of butter.

3 Heat the raisins and orange juice in a saucepan until bubbling gently.

4 Remove the pan from the heat, and leave to cool.

5 Put the flour into a large mixing bowl, and then use a wooden spoon to stir in the oats.

6 Add the butter, sugar and golden syrup to the raisins in the cooled pan.

7 Heat the pan gently, stirring until the butter and sugar are combined.

8 Ask an adult to help you tip the hot pan contents into the mixing bowl with the oats and flour. Then stir everything together, until completely mixed. This is the cookie dough.

9 Place tablespoons of the dough onto the greased baking sheets, leaving a space between each cookie. Use the back of the spoon to flatten slightly.

10 Bake for 12 to 15 minutes, or until golden. Allow to cool on the baking sheet for a few minutes, then transfer to a wire rack to cool completely. Yum!

Ballet Time

Have you ever wanted to go to ballet class? Get your dancing shoes on and figure out how to solve these puzzles. But be warned, some of them are more difficult than others. Turn to page 60 for all the answers.

WORDSEARCH

Can you find the six ballet words in the text?

ARABESQUE   LEOTARD
BALLERINA   TUTU
DANCE   PIROUETTE

N	M	F	C	Y	Z	T	S	Y	E
Y	C	L	E	O	T	A	R	D	U
X	P	G	P	K	J	Q	S	J	Q
W	G	A	O	D	X	O	N	B	S
B	A	L	L	E	R	I	N	A	E
I	G	W	T	D	U	V	U	H	B
W	Y	U	A	N	D	H	U	U	A
Z	T	N	W	B	M	V	V	Y	R
U	C	S	W	W	P	V	N	C	A
E	T	T	E	U	O	R	I	P	B

TIARA TWINS

Two of these sparkly tiaras are the same, but which two?

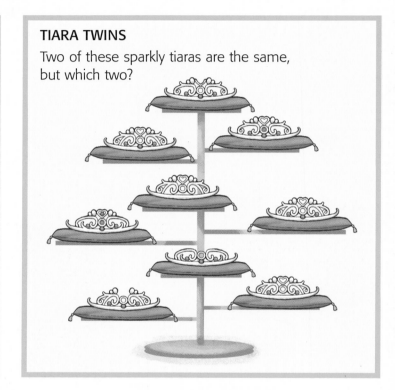

PRIMA BALLERINA

This teacher is trying to teach her pupils a new pose, but which one is copying her exactly?

BALLET MUDDLE

These girls need to find their ballet kit before they are late for class.
Help them out by following the lines.

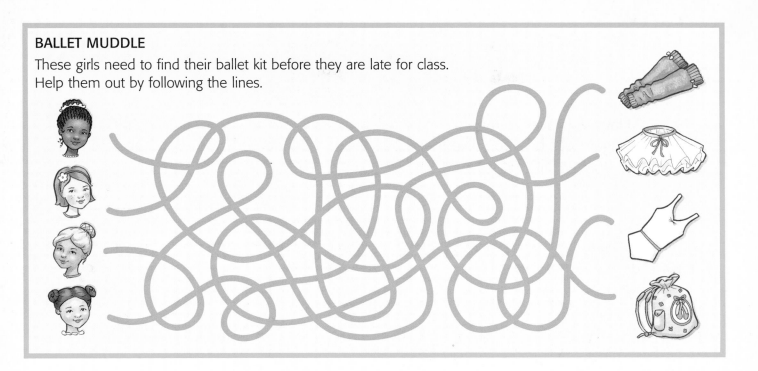

STAGE SPOT

See if you can guess
which four details to
the right are from the
stage scene below.

HOLIDAY DETECTIVES

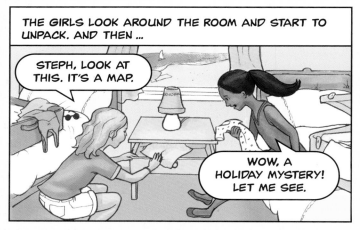

THE GIRLS RACE BACK TO THE SHOP ...

WE'VE FOUND THE TREASURE!

WELL DONE GIRLS. FAY WANTED THE PERSON WHO FOUND THE TREASURE TO KEEP A PAIR OF PEARL HAIR CLIPS ...

HERE THEY ARE. YOU DESERVE A REWARD AFTER ALL YOUR HARD WORK.

ARE YOU SURE? IT'S VERY KIND OF YOU ...

SUDDENLY, THE CURTAIN AT THE BACK OF THE SHOP OPENS ...

HI! DID YOU LIKE MY TREASURE HUNT?

MY GOODNESS! FAY, I HAD NO IDEA YOU WERE BEHIND THERE.

EVERYONE BURST OUT LAUGHING ...

HI FAY. YES, WE LOVED THE TREASURE HUNT.

ACTUALLY, WE WERE WONDERING IF YOU WANTED TO HELP US MAKE ONE OF OUR OWN?

OF COURSE I WILL. WE CAN MAKE THE MAP FOR THE NEXT GIRLS WHO COME TO THE HOTEL.

GREAT, LET'S GET STARTED!

THE GIRLS LEAVE TO PREPARE A NEW MYSTERY ...

Star Sleepover

Sleepovers are a great chance to have fun with your friends. Why not try out a pop-star theme? Follow the steps below to organize an evening of fun, games and celebrity antics.

Pop-star Sleepover

GUEST LIST

First of all, follow the instructions below to make these rockin' invites for your guests.

1. Find a close-up of each of your friends' favourite singers. Then, cut each picture out in a soft heart shape around the face.

2. Cut a piece of pink card so it will fit inside an old CD case, and glue on the head shot.

3. Once the glue has dried, use a thick red pen to draw a love heart around the picture. Next, write 'Pop-star Sleepover' at the top.

4. On the back of the card, write the time and date of your sleepover, and ask your guests to bring a pair of sunglasses and some cool clothes for dressing-up.

ALTERNATIVE: You could use a permanent marker to write the name of each guest and the sleepover details on old CDs.

5. Finally, pop the card into an empty CD case.

STAR TURN

Play this game and take turns to dress each other like a pop-star.

1. One person acts as the stylist and one as the model. The stylist has to try and make the model look like a famous pop star.

2. Try using old ties as belts, and add crazy hair clips, sunglasses and bling (time to raid your jewellery box).

3. When you've finished styling, everyone has to try and guess which pop star you've created.

4. After ten guesses, if nobody gets the right answer, you switch places and let someone else act as the stylist and model.

SINGING STAR

You need a CD player for this game. Everyone takes turns to sing along to a song of their choice, and one of you needs to act as the DJ each time.

1. The DJ starts the tune and the 'pop star' starts singing along.

2. A little way into the song, the DJ turns down the volume but the singer has to keep singing.

3. After about 20 seconds, the DJ should turn the music back up, and see if the singer is at the same point in the song as the CD.

4. The person closest to the same point as the CD is the winner.

POP GUESS WHO?

You'll need some sticky notes and pens.

1. Each player takes a sticky note and writes the name of a famous pop star on it.

2. Then you mix up the notes and turn them over so no one can see the names.

3. Without looking, everyone takes a note and sticks it on their forehead.

4. You each get a turn to ask a question, to try to find out who you are. For example, you could start with, 'Am I American?'

5. Your friends can only answer 'yes' or 'no' to your questions.

6. The first person to guess who they are wins.

MAKE A MUSIC VIDEO

Split into two groups for this game. If you have two CD players, go into separate rooms. If not, stay on different sides of the same room.

1. Play a track that everyone loves.

2. Each team has to come up with a dance routine to the song playing. Be as silly as you like, but be careful – it's easy to knock stuff over when you're dancing like crazy!

3. When you're finished, both groups take it in turns to perform their dance. The group with the best dance routine wins.

TIP: Ask someone like a mum or a big sister to pick the winning team.

Swimming Gala

These girls are having a lot of fun and getting good exercise. Look closely at the scene below.

SPOT THE DIFFERENCE

The girls are swimming fast and the crowd is cheering, but something isn't right.
See if you can spot 15 differences between the two pictures. Some of them are
tricky to find, so keep your eyes peeled! You'll find the answers on page 61.

Palm Reading

Some people believe that you can find out lots about your personality and even predict your future by studying your palm. Why not look at your right hand and have a go yourself?

1 HEART LINE

This line runs across the top of your palm. Look at it very closely. If you see a little fork at the beginning of the line (near your index finger), that means you're probably a happy person who likes to keep busy. If there's a fork at the end of the line (near your little finger), then you might be lucky. Is the line deep and easy to see? If so, then you are probably a kind-hearted person, who takes care of others.

Look closely ... sometimes lines are very faint.

2 SUN LINE

This line can be found running down your palm, sometimes between your fourth and third finger. It can be tricky to spot, and some people can't find it at all. If you can see the line clearly, that means you're likely to be sensitive. If it's long and runs all the way down to your wrist, that could mean you are independent and good at getting things done by yourself.

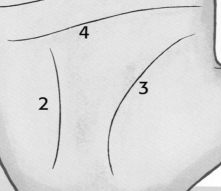

3 LIFE LINE

Look closely at your palm, near your thumb. The life line runs down here. Don't worry, it doesn't tell you how long you're going to live! If it's a clear line, then you probably have lots of energy and like to spend time with friends. If it's fainter, you might be a little more shy.

4 HEAD LINE

Remember where your heart line was? The head line runs across your palm underneath it. If the line is quite short, chances are you're good at standing up for yourself. If the line starts near your first finger, you're probably great at being organized and sorting things out. Is the head line very long? If so, you're a creative type and might end up doing something artistic in the future.

5 BRACELET LINE

This line goes across your wrist, just where a bracelet would. A very clear line suggests you're super healthy. Don't worry if the line isn't very clear though, it just means you may not be as active and sporty as some people.

Hand Massage

A hand massage feels great and is really relaxing. Why not invite a friend over and try the steps below on each other's hands? You could even give each other a manicure afterwards, so that your hands look as lovely as they feel.

1 Ask your friend to close her eyes and softly rub a blob of moisturizer all over both of her hands.

2 Take her right hand with the palm facing up and gently push the wrist upwards and back, so you're slowly letting her hand flop forwards and backwards.

3 Using your thumb and index finger, press each of your friend's fingers from tip to bottom. Hold the fingers one by one and pull them to stretch gently.

4 Turn your friend's hand over, so you can work on the back of her hand. Use your thumb to gently stroke lines from her wrist, all the way up to the tips of her fingers.

5 Turn her hand over again and use your thumb to press little circles into the palm of her hand. Now take her left hand and start again at step two.

6 Finish with another blob of moisturizer on each hand and massage in gently. Ask your friend to take a deep breath and open her eyes.

Play some soft music in the background for a peaceful mood.

DID YOU KNOW?

Some people believe that the shape of your hand can say something about the kind of person you are. If you have long slim fingers, you might be an emotional and thoughtful type. A wide palm and short fingers suggest someone who is active and sometimes a little impatient. A slim palm means you're likely to be sensitive and sympathetic. Plus, if all the lines on your hand are clear and easy-peasy to spot, chances are you're a good leader.

Get Organized!

Follow the steps below to make some marvellous matchbox drawers to stash jewellery, rings or hairpins.

You Will Need:

* Eight empty matchboxes
* PVA glue
* Thin, coloured or patterned card
* Scissors
* Acrylic paint
* A small paintbrush
* Eight small beads
* Four large beads
* A ruler

Ask an adult to find the matchboxes for you.

1 Glue the matchboxes together, one on top of the other, in two stacks of four.

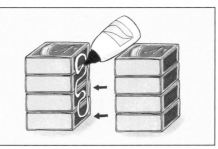

2 Spread glue all over the side of one stack, then press the other against it to stick the two piles of matchboxes together.

3 Leave the glue to dry. While you are waiting, measure the width of the drawers with the ruler. This will help with the next step.

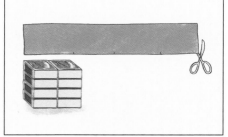

4 Cut a piece of card that's the same width as your matchbox drawers and long enough to wrap all the way around the outside.

5 Stick the card neatly in place to decorate and disguise the edges of the boxes.

6 Pull out the 'drawer' part of each matchbox, and paint. Make sure the paint is completely dry before putting the drawers back into the stacked chest.

7 Stick a small bead to the front of each drawer with blobs of glue. Leave to dry completely.

8 Stick four larger beads to the base of the chest, one near each corner, to create short, round legs. Leave the chest upside down until the glue has dried.

Top Tips

✳ Wrap a piece of sticky tape around the outside of your matchbox stacks to hold them firmly together as the glue dries. The tape will be completely hidden by the decorative card added in step five.

✳ Have a go at arranging the matchboxes in different ways. You can make a tall, thin organizer by sticking eight matchboxes in a stack, or a flat version by gluing four boxes in a row with another four on top.

✳ You can use small matchboxes or large matchboxes, depending on what you want to keep inside the drawers. Choose one size and stick to it.

✳ Decorate the outside of your chest further by sticking on glitter, sequins, lace or fabric flowers.

Organize Your Room

The matchbox drawers will help you store small items and stop them from becoming clutter, but what about the rest of your room? The ideas below will help you organize your stuff, so you'll always be able to find things in a hurry.

CLEAR OUT CLUTTER

Go through your things and get rid of anything which is broken or worn out. Then keep asking yourself the question, 'Do I really need that?' If you don't think you will ever use or wear something again, it is best to ask an adult to take it to a charity shop or give it away.

TIDY YOUR CLOTHES

Tidying your clothes can save a lot of time when you are choosing what to wear. You might even discover a really cool outfit you had forgotten all about. Put everything on clothes hangers or folded neatly into drawers. Line your shoes up in pairs along the bottom of your wardrobe. Now sort your clothes into sections of tops, trousers, skirts and dresses. If you want to be super-organized, sort them by colour as well.

ORGANIZE BOOKS AND CDS

Sort out cluttered bookcases and CD racks by organizing your books and CDs alphabetically by author or singer. You will always be able to find exactly what you're looking for.

STASH EXTRA STUFF

Decorate some shoe boxes with poster paint or wrapping paper and store anything extra inside them. This way, you can remove things from the floor and tidy them neatly under your bed or in your wardrobe. You can stick a label on each box to remind you what's inside.

Style Swap

Trying out a new look can make you feel great. Why not organize a clothes swap with a friend for some fashion fun? Follow the style tips below to make each other look really different.

GET SWAPPING

1. Ask permission from your parents to give a friend some clothes you don't wear any more and get her to do the same.

2. Take it in turns to style each other with the clothes you are allowed to give. You need to pick out an outfit, give a makeover and do each other's hair.

3. The rule is that the stylist has control and you cannot see yourself in a mirror until she has finished.

4. Use the style ideas on this page, and try out some of your own.

DRESS IN A GIRLIE STYLE

Make your friend look gorgeously girlie:

* Try dresses or skirts in pastel colours such as pink, white or pale yellow.
* Brush her hair and clip up a small section with some sparkly hair clips.
* Put some pretty pink gloss on her lips.
* Add a dainty necklace, bracelet or earrings.

ROCK-STAR STYLE

Here's how to style your friend the rock-star way:

* Dress her in dark colours, such as black and purple.
* Backcomb sections of her hair if it is straight, and add some rock-star volume.
* Give her glamorous eyes by using glittery eyeshadow.
* Rest some sunglasses on top of her head.

COLOURFUL DRESSING

Give your friend's look a burst of colour:

* Choose clashing colours when picking out an outfit, for example a yellow top and a red skirt or trousers.
* Try clothes with pretty patterns or bold logos.
* Add colourful jewellery, hair bands or grips.
* Use bright make-up on your friend's eyes or lips.

Gossip Girl

Can you keep a secret, or do you love gossip too much to stay quiet? Grab a pencil and paper and try this revealing quiz. It will tell you lots about yourself.

1. You know what your sister is getting for her birthday. Do you tell her?
A. No way! It should be a surprise for her.
B. Definitely. It's impossible to keep this to yourself.
C. Maybe – if she promised to act surprised when she opens the present …

2. You overhear your friend whispering to another mate. Do you listen in?
A. Of course not – it's obvious she doesn't want anyone else to hear.
B. Yes, you might hear some juicy gossip.
C. Maybe, but only if you thought your friend was upset and you could help.

3. Your science teacher has a new diamond ring on her finger. What do you do?
A. Wonder if she's getting married, but decide to keep it to yourself.
B. Shout so the class can hear, 'Are you engaged, Miss?'
C. Mention it to your friends after class.

4. Your friend is mega upset after a row with her mum. What do you do?
A. Bake a batch of cute cupcakes to make her smile. If she wants to talk about it, she can, but you won't ask her for details.
B. Ask her to tell you exactly what happened – it's good to talk, and you sort of want to know.
C. You ask her if she wants to talk about it, but completely understand if she'd rather not chat.

5. Your friend admits she still sleeps with her teddy bear. What do you do?
A. Keep it to yourself, and don't talk about it. She's probably quite embarrassed.
B. Think it's funny and tell everyone about it. She can take a joke!
C. Tell her there's nothing wrong with that. Teddy bears are cuddly.

Now it's time to find out which ones you've ticked most often. Add up how many As, Bs and Cs you have chosen and turn to page 61.

Heart Pendants

You spend every day with your best friend. You can talk to her about anything and she always makes you laugh. Plus, you're so similar, that people often mistake you for sisters. Why not show her how special she is by making these pretty friendship pendants?

You Will Need:

* 200 g plain flour
* 100 g table salt
* 175 ml water
* Lemon juice
* A rolling pin
* A heart-shaped cookie-cutter
* Narrow ribbon
* A cocktail stick, or knitting needle
* A small brush
* Acrylic paint
* Scissors

1 Put the flour, salt and two or three drops of lemon juice in a bowl.

2 Gradually stir in the cold water. The mixture should become a stiff dough.

WARNING

Always ask an adult to help you when using an oven. Use oven gloves when putting things in the oven and taking them out.

3 Next, knead the dough. It shouldn't be too sticky, and it should be soft enough to stretch easily. If it seems too dry, you'll need to add more water. If you think it is too wet, add more flour.

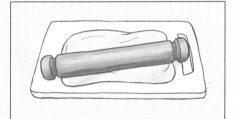

4 Smooth a thin layer of flour over a chopping board or flat surface. Then roll the dough out until it is about 5 mm thick.

5 Using the cookie-cutter, cut out two heart shapes to make the pendants. Be careful of your fingers!

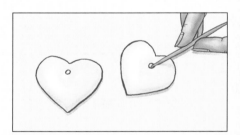

6 Scrape out a round hole near the top of each heart, using a cocktail stick or a knitting needle.

7 Bake the hearts for three hours at 120°C/250°F/Gas Mark 2. Leave them to cool in the oven for four or five minutes, then put them on a wire rack to cool completely.

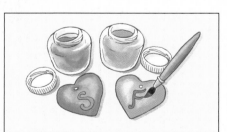

8 Paint the hearts with acrylic paint, each in a different colour. Leave to dry, and then paint your initial on one and your best friend's initial on the other.

9 Cut a length of ribbon, fold it in half, and push through the pendant hole. Then pull the ribbon ends through the loop.

10 Tie one pendant around your neck and give the other to your best friend.

TIP
Brush a coat of clear nail polish on to your finished pendant for a super-glossy, varnished look.

DID YOU KNOW?

The charms below are given as gifts of friendship, and they bring good luck, too.

CELTIC KNOT
This is a pretty knot which can be worn as jewellery. It symbolises unity, strength and unbreakable friendship.

TURQUOISE
A turquoise gemstone offers protection. Give it to a friend to help shield them from harm and show them you care.

The Friendship Test

Find out how much you know about each other. Write your friend's name in the box on the left, then answer the questions about her. Your best friend does the same for you in the box on the right, then you both correct each other. If each of you gets four or more questions right, you are true friends.

NAME: ....   NAME: ....

Her favourite food is … .... ○ YES ○ NO   .... ○ YES ○ NO

Her favourite colour is … .... ○ YES ○ NO   .... ○ YES ○ NO

Her favourite TV show is … .... ○ YES ○ NO   .... ○ YES ○ NO

Her favourite animal is … .... ○ YES ○ NO   .... ○ YES ○ NO

Her favourite hobby is … .... ○ YES ○ NO   .... ○ YES ○ NO

Her favourite subject is … .... ○ YES ○ NO   .... ○ YES ○ NO

Her favourite outfit is … .... ○ YES ○ NO   .... ○ YES ○ NO

Her future job will be … .... ○ YES ○ NO   .... ○ YES ○ NO

Superstar Game

Grab a few friends and get set for the best board game around.

HOW TO PLAY

You can play with just two people or with as many as five, it's up to you. All you need is one dice and a counter each – use a button, a coin, or anything else you have to hand. Take turns rolling the dice. Whoever rolls a six first gets to start. Then each time you roll the dice, move your counter the number of spaces shown. Whoever makes it to the end first is the superstar winner.

START HERE

Uh-oh! Your teeny lapdog has weed all over your limo. Go back three spaces.

You manage to walk the red carpet in super-high heels. Move on two spaces.

You forget your lines during a rehearsal – go back one space.

You've got a designer dress for the biggest party in town. Move on three spaces.

A celebrity invites you to a pool party. Move on two spaces.

You get a pile of fan mail. How nice! Move on one space.

HOLLYWOOD

Your fave boy celeb asks you to a black-tie ball. Move on two spaces.

You fall over at an awards ceremony. Roll an even number to move on.

You chill out at the beach, but step on a jellyfish. Go back three spaces.

A famous female actress takes you for ice cream. Move on two spaces.

Everyone is copying your new jeans. Move on one space.

Oh man. You spill an ice-cream sundae all over a supermodel. Go back five.

You have a hair disaster and the paparazzi get a snap of you looking scruffy. Go back two spaces.

Your private limo has broken down. You'll have to miss a turn.

You forget to take the tag off your new dress when you wear it to the Oscars. Go back two.

You are generous and fly your whole family to LA for a movie premiere. Roll again.

You go to Hawaii to work on a top-secret film set. Move on three spaces.

YOU WIN! Congratulations on being the coolest celeb in the world.

HAWAII

Tea Party

Edwardian ladies had fancy tea parties throughout the year.
Everyone wore a beautiful dress, ate cake and drank tea. Here's how to throw your own.

SEND INVITATIONS

First, you need to tell your friends about your tea party and ask them to come. Turn to page 50 to create pretty handmade invitations. You will find a template of a teapot to copy, with blanks for you to fill in important information such as the date, time and address. Then you are all set to have fun.

YUMMY FOOD

Sandwiches and cakes are the best food to eat at tea parties.

* Mini sandwiches with the crusts cut off will look lovely on your table and they taste good, too. Try making them with cucumber or tuna, or ham and cheese, then cut them into little triangles.
* You could also put a bowl of crisps on the table for everyone to share. They make a great snack.
* Turn to page 51 to make a delicious cheesecake and impress your guests.

MAKE A PERFECT CUP OF TEA

Ask an adult to help you, and follow these steps:

* Fill the kettle up with water and turn it on.
* When boiled, pour a small amount of hot water into the teapot, swirl it around, and tip out to warm the pot.
* Put three or four teabags into the teapot.
* Fill up the teapot with hot water.
* Put the lid on the pot and leave to brew for three minutes.
* Finally, add a splash of milk to a cup, and then pour in the tea, holding the teapot lid to stop it falling off.

SET THE TABLE

If it is sunny, why not ask an adult if you can sit outside? It will feel like you are at a real Edwardian garden party. Don't worry if you need to stay indoors though, there is still plenty of fun to be had. Here's how to get the table ready:

1. Lay a pretty tablecloth over the top.
2. Put a teapot, sugar bowl and milk jug in the centre.
3. Set a plate opposite each chair.
4. Place a folded napkin, spoon and fork next to each plate.
5. Put a cup and saucer to the top right of each plate.

GARDEN PARTY GAMES

People in the early 20th century often held tea parties in their gardens or went on picnics in the summer. After everyone had finished eating, they sometimes played games. You might like to try playing some too:

✳ BLIND MAN'S BUFF. This game is the same as Tag, but the catcher is in the dark. This makes it extra fun. To play, one of you wears a blindfold and has to catch everyone else. If you are caught, it is your turn to wear the blindfold and do the catching.

✳ KIM'S GAME. Place a selection of 15 household objects on a tray. The objects need to be small, such as a fridge magnet, a torch or an orange. Each player has one minute to memorize the items, before the tray gets covered with a cloth. Then players need to write down on a piece of paper all the items they can remember. A point is scored for each item remembered correctly, but a point is lost for any which were never there.

COLOUR THE PICTURE

It is a beautiful summer's day and these three Edwardian ladies are enjoying tea in the garden. Complete the picture by adding colour. You can use pens, pencils or even paint. It's up to you.

You're Invited!

You learnt how to throw an old-fashioned tea party on pages 48 and 49, so now you need to send invitations. A text, email or phone call is a modern way to invite guests, but it doesn't fit with the Edwardian mood. Why not follow the instructions below instead?

Make Your Own Invitations

Trace the pretty teapot below onto a piece of thick coloured card. Fill in the date and time, and put your name alongside 'hostess'. Where it says 'place', you will need to write your full address and phone number. Use your best handwriting and a coloured pen to make your invitations really special.

TRACING TIPS

Place a sheet of tracing paper over the teapot below, and use a ballpoint pen to draw over the picture outline. Turn the tracing paper over, and scribble over the lines you have just drawn with a soft-lead pencil. Next, tape the tracing paper, with the pencil-scribble side down, onto a piece of thick coloured card. Draw over the outline of the teapot again with the pen. When you remove the tracing paper, you will see the imprint of the teapot on the card. Cut around this to make your invitation. Repeat until you have all the invitations you need.

DID YOU KNOW?

R.S.V.P. stands for 'répondez, s'il vous plaît'. That's French for 'Respond, if you please'. If you see that on an invitation, it means you should reply and let the hostess know if you will be coming or not. Sometimes fancy invitations to very big parties say 'Regrets Only'. This means you only need to reply if you can't attend.

Come To My Tea Party

DATE...

TIME...

HOSTESS ....

PLACE ....

....

TEL ....

R.S.V.P.

Lemon Cheesecake

Here is a recipe to make a delicious lemon cheesecake. You will need to use a springform cake tin to make it. This is a special tin, which has a catch at the side, so you can easily get the cake out once it is ready.

INGREDIENTS

200 g digestive biscuits
60 g butter
1 lemon
300 g medium fat
  cream cheese
75 g caster sugar
150 ml double cream

Ask an adult to help you use the hob.

1 Put the biscuits into a food bag, and crush into crumbs with a rolling pin.

2 Put the butter in a saucepan and melt it on the hob, over a low heat.

3 Remove the pan from the hob.

4 Add the biscuit crumbs to the melted butter and stir using a wooden spoon, until completely mixed.

5 Tip the mixture into a 20 cm springform cake tin. Use the bottom of a glass to flatten, and chill in the refrigerator for around 20 minutes.

6 Wash the lemon and grate the zest into a bowl. Make sure you do not include any of the white pith.

7 Now cut the lemon in half and squeeze out the juice.

8 Place the cream cheese in a mixing bowl and add the sugar. Beat until mixed together, and then whisk in the double cream.

9 Pour in the lemon juice and zest, and whisk until thick and creamy.

10 Make sure the biscuit base is properly chilled, then remove it from the refrigerator.

11 Pour the cream-cheese mixture on top of the biscuit base, and spread it out evenly.

12 Put the cake in the refrigerator to chill for a couple of hours. This allows it to set properly.

13 Unclip and remove the cake tin. Your cake is ready to serve. Cut it into slices, and enjoy.

Spot The Fakes

One of these five stories is true, but can you guess which one? The answer is on page 61.

BIZARRE BEANS

In 1945 two sisters found some mysterious beans in the back garden of their home in Tennessee. They had read the story of *Jack and the Beanstalk*, and so they decided to plant the beans at the end of the garden. To their astonishment, a beanstalk appeared the very next day, and over the next few weeks it grew to the amazing height of three metres. Sadly, the beanstalk wasn't magical, but everyone in the area was completely amazed. Not only did the girls' strange beanstalk win first prize in the state fair, the story even made *The New York Times*!

TRUE OR FALSE?

AMAZING ALIENS

In 1980 a family in Germany saw some strange red lights flashing in the sky above their house. The lights got closer and closer, and then suddenly a large object reared into view. It was shaped like a huge disk, and there was a dome at the top, just like a UFO. The family watched in horror as it fell down towards them. It was going to crash! They ducked and the enormous disk hit their roof. Fortunately, it only skimmed over the surface, knocking off a few tiles. When the family looked up into the sky again, it was gone.

TRUE OR FALSE?

PLANE DRAMA

In 1999, a ten-year-old girl surprised the world when she managed to land a passenger plane. The plane got into difficulties when the pilot passed out due to food poisoning. Ten-year-old Jessica White stepped up, having read about planes for a recent school project. Helping the co-pilot, she managed to keep calm and assist him as he brought the plane down in a field. The whole plane came down safely and the passengers only suffered bumps and bruises.

TRUE OR FALSE?

FAKE FAIRIES

In 1917, two young girls living in Yorkshire, England, amazed the country when they took photos of fairies in their back garden. Word spread, and soon photograph experts were taking a look. The photos were made into slides and shown at a lecture in London, and the buzz grew so much that the girls' pictures made the front page of a magazine. The publication sold out within days.

Eventually, 36 years later, one of the girls admitted that the photographs were a hoax, claiming that they had drawn the fairies, cut them out and fastened them to the ground with hatpins. But the girls had still managed to trick thousands of people.

TRUE OR FALSE?

DARING RAID

In 1965, a gang of burglars made off with a bag full of diamonds in one of the most daring crimes ever. Three young women managed to sneak into Buckingham Palace disguised as servants. They spent an entire night in the palace without being caught, and shortly after 4 am, they sneaked into the Queen's private dressing room and managed to steal over one million pounds' worth of jewellery. The burglars even made it out as far as the palace gates, before being nabbed by a sentry on duty. Talk about being caught red-handed!

TRUE OR FALSE?

❧ Rainforest Fun ❧

Hang some binoculars round your neck, because it's time to go on safari.
Take a tour of the rainforest and solve these puzzles. You'll find the answers on page 61.

TREE-FROG SPOT THE DIFFERENCE

See if you can spot five differences between these colourful tree frogs.

FROG FACT Tree frogs have big, bright-red eyes to scare off predators.

FRUIT-BAT COUNT

There are 30 fruit bats in this picture. Can you spot them all?

SAFARI DOT-TO-DOT

Join the dots to find out which animal is climbing in the tree. Find out on page 61.

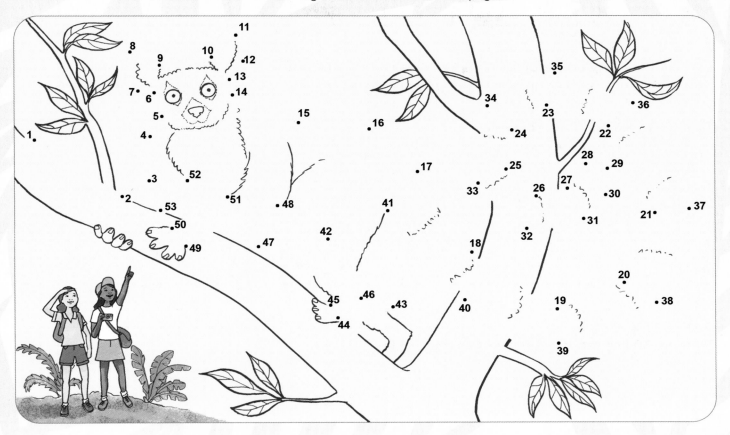

SQUIRREL-MONKEY SUDOKU

Arrange the squirrel-monkey's food so that every row, column and each of the four coloured squares contains a banana, nuts, a mango and leaves. Can you draw the pictures in the correct squares to complete the grid?

MONKEY FACT

Monkeys move easily in the treetops by using their tails to grab onto branches and help them balance.

Emergency Kit

Everyone feels sad sometimes, and this is when you need a friend to be there for you and help cheer you up. If your friend is feeling blue, why not make her a special present? Simply follow the steps below, and whatever the emergency, this little box is guaranteed to make her smile.

You Will Need:

* A shoe box
* Red, white and black poster paint
* A paintbrush
* Tissue paper
* Old newspaper
* Small gifts

You can choose paints in different colours if you prefer.

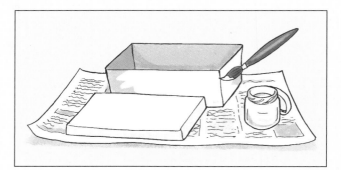

1 Lay some newspaper down, and paint the outside of the shoebox and the lid with white poster paint. Leave the white paint to dry.

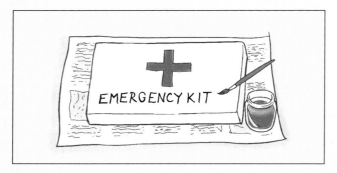

2 Once the white paint is dry, paint a red cross on top of the lid. Then, underneath the cross, paint the words 'EMERGENCY KIT' in black paint.

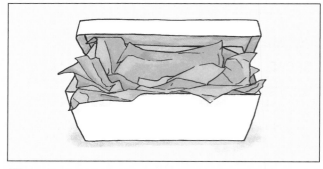

3 Fill the inside of the box with tissue paper to make it look pretty.

4 Now your Emergency Kit is ready to be filled with small presents. There are lots of suggestions on the next page.

GIGGLES GUARANTEED!

Copy these jokes and put them in the box to make your friend laugh.
* What do you call a bee that always complains?
A grumble bee
* What is a frog's favourite winter sport?
Ice hoppy
* What cheese is made backwards?
Edam

FRIENDSHIP BRACELET

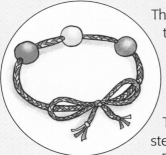

This bracelet is very simple to make and will show your friend how much you care. All you need is three different-coloured threads and a few beads. Then follow the simple steps opposite and pop it in your Emergency Kit.

1. Cut the three pieces of thread to a length of 20 cm.
2. Bunch them together and tie a knot at one end.
3. Plait the three threads, starting at the knot and going all the way down.
4. Push a couple of beads onto the plait.
5. Tie a knot at the other end.
6. Tie the bracelet in a bow around your friend's wrist.

SMILE-WORTHY EXTRAS

You could also try filling the Emergency Kit with the following items:
* A chocolate bar.
* A CD by her favourite band.
* Photographs of the two of you having fun. Make her laugh by including some where you both look silly!
* Nail varnish in her favourite colour.

MY FRIEND IS GREAT…

Why not write a list of words to describe how special your friend is? You can pick some words from the list below or write some of your own.

Kind	Clever
Thoughtful	Pretty
Happy	Loyal
Funny	Caring
Giggly	Stylish

The Perfect Day

Ever fancied writing your own story? Here's your chance. Whenever you see a blank, it's up to you to fill it in. Sometimes you get a selection of words in brackets to choose from, but most of the time you can write whatever you like. Afterwards, find out what your unique story says about you.

Once upon a time there was a very cool girl called _____. For her birthday, she got to go on an amazing shopping trip with her best friend _____.

At the mall they headed straight for _____ where they bought lots of amazing _____. After they had finished shopping, they had more fun at the _____ (cinema/ice rink/bowling alley). They rounded off their special day with a yummy _____ (pizza, milkshake, ice cream).

When they got back to _____ 's home in the sunny town of _____, there was a pile of birthday cards plus one important-looking letter.

'I wonder what this is?' _____ asked, and tore open the envelope. Nervously, she read the letter inside and gave a shriek of joy, 'I've won!' A few weeks ago, she had entered a competition on TV, where the winner would get a wish granted for one day. She had always wanted to be a famous _____ (ballerina/actress/fashion designer/writer), but she never thought she would win! Now, for one very special day, she could _____ (dance on stage/act in a TV soap/design an outfit/get a book published).

On the day, a chauffeur-driven car came to collect her and take her to the _____ (theatre/TV set/fashion house/publisher).

Everyone was really friendly and _____ had the best day of her life. She impressed everyone with her brilliant _____ (dancing/acting/designs/short stories) and they told her to come and visit them again soon.

The next morning _____ woke up and wondered if it had all been an incredible dream. But then she saw her _____ (ballet shoes/VIP studio pass/designer dress/book of short stories) and she knew it had actually happened.

There was a knock on her bedroom door, and her mum came in, carrying a tray with orange juice and a delicious cooked breakfast. Tucked underneath the plate was a copy of the local newspaper.

'I think you'll want to see this,' laughed her mum, handing her the paper. It was amazing. Right there on the front page, was her story. The headline read:

LOCAL GIRL _____ (TAKES TO THE STAGE/FILMS WITH THE STARS/PRESENTS HER DESIGNS/PUBLISHES BOOK OF STORIES)

She was famous. She threw her arms around her mum. 'I guess that just proves that girls can do anything,' she said smiling, before tucking into her delicious breakfast.

Personality Profile
What do your choices say about you?

✳ If you went for the chance to be a **ballerina**, it means you are likely to be graceful and super-fit, with big ambitions. You love the idea of the spotlight, but you know it takes lots of hard work. This doesn't bother you as you'd be willing to work for fame.

✳ If you went for the chance to be an **actress**, you're probably confident and independent, with a real flair for drama. You wouldn't mind being a celebrity – you'd just pop on your dark glasses and sign as many autographs as your fans wanted.

✳ If you picked the chance to be a **fashion designer**, you're probably a creative chick with lots of cool artistic ideas. It goes without saying you've got fabulous style … you probably do a brilliant job of giving your mates fashion advice already.

✳ If you chose to be a **writer**, you are likely to be very imaginative with big ideas. You are a dreamer, and you love thinking about the world and inventing stories. You don't want to be famous for the sake of it, you want to be admired for your talent.

Answers

Pages 28 to 29

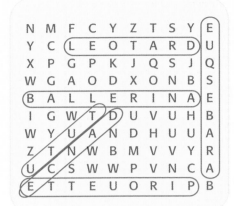

Pages 10 to 11

Mostly As: Cool Cat

You are a chilled girl who loves relaxing and listening to music. Sometimes you are a little shy and you don't enjoy taking on too many activities at once. You are an individual, but you always make time for the people you care about.

Mostly Bs: Girly Girl

You like anything cute and cuddly, and you're the best person to give out hugs in a crisis. You know how to kick back and relax, but you throw a great sleepover and give great fashion advice. You don't like sport but you could shop for hours.

Mostly Cs: A Get-Up-And-Go Girl

You're definitely a go-girl – full of energy all the time! You don't like having to sit around when you could be up and about doing things or playing your favourite sports. You're a fab friend because you're always up for trying new things.

Page 17

Pages 36 to 37

Page 43

Mostly As: Secret Star
You're not a big gossip and you always respect everyone else's space. If someone shares a secret with you, there's no way you would ever tell. That's fantastic, but remember, it's OK to talk to your friends when there's something you want to share.

Mostly Bs: Gossip Girl
You're loads of fun and you love a good chat. You're not very good at keeping secrets, because you just can't resist sharing the gossip. It might be fun to spill the beans, but remember your friends might want to keep the odd secret quiet.

Mostly Cs: Chatty Chick
You're a really good mate – always happy to talk over a friend's problem or have a bit of a gossip, but without being nosy. Good for you! There's nothing wrong with the occasional bit of chat, especially if it brings you closer to your mates.

Pages 52 to 53

The true story is the *Fake Fairies* story.
Did you guess right?

Pages 54 to 55

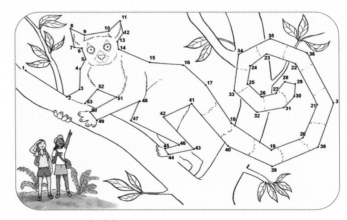

It's a ring-tailed lemur